THE ChatGPT MILLIONAIRE MANIFESTO

UNVEILING THE MIND-BLOWING **WEALTH SECRETS** OF CHATGPT

MIA CASHMAN

Copyright © by 2023 Envision Global Press

All rights reserved. No part of this book may be reproduced or transmitted in any form, by any means mechanical or electronic, including photocopying, duplicating, recording or by any information storage and retrieval system, without prior permission in writing from the publisher and copyright holders.

Table of Contents

Introduction 1
Chapter 1: The Revolution of Bitcoin 4
Chapter 2: The Genesis of Bitcoin: A Brief History 8
Chapter 3: Blockchain Explained: The Engine Behind Bitcoin 12
Chapter 4: The Psychology of Cryptocurrency: Why Bitcoin Matters 16
Chapter 5: Setting Up Your Bitcoin Wallet: Your First Steps 20
Chapter 6: Understanding Bitcoin Exchanges: Where to Buy and Sell 25
Chapter 7: Basic Trading Techniques: Tips and Strategies for Beginners 30
Chapter 8: Advanced Trading Techniques: Taking Your Portfolio to New Heights 33
Chapter 9: Security Measures: Protecting Your Digital Wealth . 36
Chapter 10: Tax Implications: Navigating the Legal Landscape 39
Chapter 11: Bitcoin Mining: The Backbone of the Network ... 42
Chapter 12: Altcoins and Tokens: The Extended Cryptocurrency Universe 46
Chapter 13: Bitcoin in Business: Revolutionizing Commerce . 49
Chapter 14: Investing Long-Term: Hodling Strategies 52
Chapter 15: The Dark Side: Risks and Scams to Avoid 55
Chapter 16: Real-World Applications: Bitcoin Beyond Trading 58
Chapter 17: Social and Cultural Impact: Changing the Global Paradigm 62
Chapter 18: Future Predictions: What Experts Say About Bitcoin's Potential 65

Chapter 19: Action Plan: Your Roadmap to Becoming a Bitcoin Millionaire 68

Chapter 20: Embracing the Crypto Lifestyle: Beyond Just Bitcoin .. 73

Chapter 21: NFTs - The New Digital Art Revolution 76

Chapter 22: DeFi - The Future of Decentralized Finance . 79

Chapter 23: The Evolution of Digital Identity 83

Chapter 24: Central Bank Digital Currencies (CBDCs) - The State's Response 87

Chapter 25: The Role of Cryptocurrencies in Philanthropy . 91

Conclusion: Reshaping Your Financial Destiny with Bitcoin . 95

Appendix A: Glossary of Bitcoin and Cryptocurrency Terms 98

Introduction

Welcome to "The Bitcoin Millionaire Manifesto: Unveiling the Mind-Blowing Wealth Secrets of Bitcoin." So, you're intrigued by Bitcoin, right? Perhaps you've heard tantalizing tales of people transforming their financial lives, seemingly overnight. Or maybe you're just fed up with the roller coaster of traditional financial systems. Whichever camp you fall into, I assure you, you're holding in your hands—or perhaps on your screen—the ultimate guide to understanding, exploring, and possibly even profiting from the world of Bitcoin.

Why is this book a must-read, you ask? Simply put, it's all about financial freedom. Let's face it, the days of relying solely on 9-to-5 jobs or traditional investments like stock and bonds are fading fast. A new wave of financial opportunities is upon us, and Bitcoin is at the forefront. This isn't just another trend; it's a financial revolution. With this book as your compass, you'll navigate through the Bitcoin universe, avoiding pitfalls and, fingers crossed, finding your own treasure along the way.

Now, let's talk about Bitcoin's revolutionary potential. Imagine a world without banks holding your money hostage, without exorbitant fees for international transactions, and without the fear of inflation eating into your savings. Sounds dreamy, doesn't it? Well, that's the world Bitcoin is striving to create—a decentralized financial universe where you hold the reins. In this world, your money isn't just a number on a bank statement but a direct expression of your financial freedom. It's not just a fad; it's the future.

You're probably wondering, "Okay, but what am I going to learn here?" Great question! You'll start with a tour of Bitcoin's early days, a gripping saga featuring enigmatic creators and radical ideas. But we won't stop at the history; we'll dive deep into the engine that powers it all: blockchain. You'll understand how to set up your Bitcoin wallet, learn the ABCs of trading, and even unearth strategies for long-term investment. If you're a business owner or aspiring entrepreneur, don't worry, there's something for you too! We'll explore how Bitcoin is revolutionizing various industries and why you should be part of it.

The book is structured to take you on a journey—from a novice scratching their head over what Bitcoin is, to a confident individual ready to make informed decisions in the Bitcoin ecosystem. We'll tackle the essentials, explore advanced strategies, discuss the cultural and social impacts, and wrap things up with actionable steps for your own Bitcoin adventure. Plus, there are exciting appendices to feed your insatiable curiosity about related topics.

So, what's the call to action? Engage, engage, engage! Don't just skim through the pages. Take notes, ask questions, be skeptical, and then seek answers—either in this book or through further research. Apply the tips and techniques, and who knows, you might be sharing your own Bitcoin success story sooner than you think.

So grab your favorite beverage, find a comfortable chair, and let's take the first step into this exciting, ever-evolving universe. Your financial future awaits, and it's brighter than ever with Bitcoin by your side.

Ready to hop on this wild ride? Let's get started!

Chapter 1:

The Revolution of Bitcoin

Ah, the wonderful, mystifying, and oh-so-talked-about world of Bitcoin! If you've ever dabbled in conversations about finance or spent way too much time scrolling through social media, you've likely heard the term tossed around. But what is Bitcoin, really? Is it a fabled treasure chest or just fool's gold? By the end of this chapter, you'll be the one at the party dropping knowledge bombs about Bitcoin's revolutionary impact on, well, just about everything.

The Disruptive Power of Bitcoin in the Financial Sector

Let's kick things off by diving into how Bitcoin is shaking up the financial sector like a salt shaker on a dining table that's never seen seasoning. You see, for the longest time, banking systems have acted like the guardians of our money. They decide who gets a loan, who pays what in transaction fees, and who can access financial services. Then Bitcoin strolled into the scene like a rebel with a cause, yelling, "No more!"

Bitcoin's decentralized nature turns the traditional financial power dynamics upside down. There's no central entity or government pulling the strings. It's like removing the king from the chessboard and letting the pawns decide their moves. You are your own bank, you set your terms, and the blockchain—a public ledger visible to everyone—

ensures transparency. Banking, meet your modern, cooler, decentralized competitor.

Social and Cultural Changes Driven by Bitcoin

Now, don't think Bitcoin's influence stops at Wall Street. Oh no, it's rippling through society like a wave you didn't see coming. Remember when we used to barter goods? Someone decided that was inefficient, and boom, currency was born. Fast forward several centuries, and Bitcoin is triggering a similar shift but on a digital plane.

Culturally, we're seeing the democratization of wealth. Before, investment opportunities in high-value assets were limited to the elite. With Bitcoin, anyone with a smartphone can participate in the global economy. Artists are now selling digital art through Bitcoin, rural farmers in developing countries are receiving fair compensation, and online communities are booming with Bitcoin as the universal currency. We're talking about a cultural revolution here!

Bitcoin vs. Traditional Currency

Time for the ultimate face-off: Bitcoin versus traditional currency! In one corner, we have good ol' paper money, backed by government promises and people's faith. In the other corner, we have Bitcoin—no government backing, but a lot of computational power and also people's faith. You might think, "Hey, I can't touch or see Bitcoin, so it must be less real, right?" Well, when was the last time you actually touched all the money you claim to have in your bank account?

Bitcoin offers advantages like lower transaction fees, especially for international dealings, and faster processing times. Plus, your Bitcoin is yours and yours alone, thanks to cryptographic keys. No more worrying about a financial institution collapsing and running off with your money.

Real-World Cases of Bitcoin Adoption

Still not convinced? Let's dish out some real-world examples of Bitcoin adoption that are as legit as your grandma's secret pasta sauce recipe. Businesses from small online stores to giant corporations are hopping onto the Bitcoin train for their transaction needs. Take Tesla, for example. They accepted Bitcoin payments for their electric cars for a while. How about countries? El Salvador made headlines when it adopted Bitcoin as legal tender, shaking the pillars of traditional finance.

The Promise and Hype Surrounding Bitcoin

To wrap up this chapter, let's chat about the sizzle around Bitcoin—the promise and the hype. Every day, headlines scream about new Bitcoin millionaires, lost keys worth a fortune, or large corporations investing heavily in it. Yes, Bitcoin promises a lot, from financial freedom to disrupting centralized systems. But remember, with great potential comes great volatility. The value of Bitcoin can swing faster than your mood on a Monday morning. Yet, this very volatility is what makes it so darn attractive to investors and risk-takers.

The buzz isn't just about getting rich quick; it's about the fundamental changes Bitcoin brings to the table. It promises a future where the world isn't reliant on fallible centralized systems, where financial power is back in the hands of the people, and where the lines between different types of currency become increasingly blurred.

So there you have it—the revolutionary spectacle that is Bitcoin. Whether you're a skeptic, a newbie, or a seasoned Bitcoiner, you can't deny the rippling impact it's making across various aspects of our lives. From finance to social norms, it's not just an alternative; it's an evolution.

Brace yourself, because the revolution is here, and it's digitized. The question is, are you ready to be a part of it?

Chapter 2:

The Genesis of Bitcoin: A Brief History

Alright, gather 'round, everyone! It's story time. Imagine the suspense of a mystery novel, the plot twists of a thriller, and the insight of a history book—all rolled into one. That's the saga of Bitcoin for you. No capes, no magic wands, but plenty of drama and enigma. So, fasten your seatbelts as we go back to where it all began, where the digital and financial realms collided in the most spectacular way. Welcome to the genesis of Bitcoin!

The White Paper and the Birth of Bitcoin

Picture it: The year is 2008, and the world is spiraling into a financial crisis. Banks are faltering, governments are scrambling, and trust in financial institutions is plummeting faster than a lead balloon. Enter a mysterious figure named Satoshi Nakamoto. No, not a character from a sci-fi movie, but the pseudonymous person (or group of people) who published a white paper called "Bitcoin: A Peer-to-Peer Electronic Cash System."

What did this nine-page document say? In layman's terms, it laid out a groundbreaking idea—a decentralized, digital currency that didn't need middlemen like banks. All it required was some heavy-duty math and a sprinkle of computer science wizardry. Within months, the Bitcoin network was born, with the release of its open-source software in 2009. Little did anyone know, it was the beginning of a revolution.

Key Milestones in Bitcoin's Development

Just like any great invention, Bitcoin had its share of Eureka moments and face palms. Let's start with the positives. In January 2009, the first-ever Bitcoin block, fondly known as the "Genesis Block," was mined. Fast forward to May 2010, and we have the infamous pizza purchase—two pizzas bought for 10,000 BTC. At today's rates, that's a ludicrously expensive meal!

Another big moment was in 2013 when Bitcoin's value first crossed the $1,000 mark. Pop the champagne, right? But wait, there were speed bumps. The platform Mt. Gox, which handled a significant portion of Bitcoin transactions, was hacked in 2014, causing the cryptocurrency's value to plummet. Lessons were learned, and security measures tightened, but it was a watershed moment for the fledgling network.

Early Adopters and Skeptics

Oh boy, the characters in the early days of Bitcoin were a mixed bag, ranging from tech geeks and libertarians to financial moguls and skeptics galore. Early adopters saw Bitcoin as the future—anonymous, decentralized, and borderless. They were the miners, the traders, and the dreamers.

On the flip side, we had the skeptics, and not just your Uncle Bob who still uses a flip phone. Established economists, financial experts, and governments around the globe questioned Bitcoin's legitimacy, viability, and security. Terms like "bubble," "fraud," and "Ponzi scheme" were thrown around more than a football during the Super Bowl. Yet, the very skepticism that sought to quash Bitcoin only fueled the fire of curiosity.

Major Events like Forks and Legal Battles

If you think Bitcoin's journey was smooth sailing, think again. A "fork" in cryptocurrency language is akin to a family feud—two sides disagreeing on the way forward. Bitcoin has experienced several forks, leading to offshoots like Bitcoin Cash and Bitcoin SV. Each fork shook the community and markets but also pushed the technology into new directions.

Legal battles? Oh, there were plenty. Regulatory crackdowns, high-profile court cases, and government bans added layers of complexity to Bitcoin's evolution. Remember Silk Road, the dark web marketplace for all things illegal? Its shutdown by the FBI in 2013 put Bitcoin under the spotlight, but also led to more robust legal frameworks.

Bitcoin's Growing Mainstream Acceptance

We've come a long way, haven't we? From techie forums and shady marketplaces, Bitcoin is now hobnobbing with the mainstream crowd. Major companies like PayPal, Square, and even Wall Street investment funds have warmed up to it. Governments, while still cautious, are exploring ways to regulate and even embrace this digital asset. Heck, even your grandma might be considering adding some BTC to her knitting fund!

So what does this all mean? Bitcoin is no longer a rebel without a cause; it's a rebel that's winning hearts, minds, and wallets. The road was far from easy, but the signs are clear: Bitcoin is here to stay.

Alright, that's a wrap for Chapter 2! What a rollercoaster, huh? And we've only just skimmed the surface. The Bitcoin iceberg is much more extensive than what's visible, and as we move forward, you'll uncover even more layers. So don't go anywhere; the next chapters are going to be a blast!

Did you find this chapter riveting? Excited about what's coming next? You should be! We've got loads more to talk about, so turn that page, swipe that screen, or do whatever you do to continue reading. Onward!

Chapter 3:

Blockchain Explained: The Engine Behind Bitcoin

Ah, welcome back! Grab your favorite snack, and let's dive back into the adventure that is the world of Bitcoin. Now, you may be thinking, "I get Bitcoin; it's digital money. But what's all this talk about blockchain?" Fear not, my friend! By the end of this chapter, you'll be tossing around the term "blockchain" like a pro, impressing your friends, family, and maybe even your dog.

Defining What a Blockchain Is

Alright, let's start with the basics. Imagine a public ledger or notebook that anyone can see and add to, but once something is written, it's there forever—indelible, unchangeable, and transparent. Welcome to the blockchain! It's a series of blocks (lists of transactions) that are chained together and secured using cryptography. This isn't just any ledger; it's a ledger on steroids! It's the brilliant technology that allows cryptocurrencies like Bitcoin to operate without a central authority. So, no more bankers in pin-striped suits calling the shots.

How Blockchain Technology Supports Bitcoin

You know how every superhero has their trusty sidekick? Well, if Bitcoin is Batman, then blockchain is Robin. Bitcoin relies on blockchain to function. When you make a Bitcoin transaction, it gets grouped with others into a block. Miners (not the pickaxe kind) then validate these transactions using complex mathematical problems. Once solved, the block is added to the existing chain of previous transactions, forming a, you guessed it, blockchain!

This process creates a public, transparent history of all transactions, making it nearly impossible to cheat the system. Just try altering a block, and you'd have to change every subsequent block in the chain. Talk about mission impossible!

The Concept of Decentralization

Now, onto a term that you'll hear more often than a catchy pop song—decentralization. In a decentralized system, no single entity or institution holds power. It's like having a classroom without a teacher, where all the kids are equally in charge and work together to maintain order (or chaos, depending on how you look at it).

In the world of blockchain, this means multiple nodes (computers) hold copies of the blockchain. For a transaction to be validated, a majority of nodes have to agree. This setup makes the system robust and democratic. Even if one or two nodes go rogue, they can't really alter the entire blockchain, thanks to the consensus of the rest. It's power to the people, 21st-century style!

Security Features of Blockchain

If blockchain were a fortress, it would make the Great Wall of China look like a picket fence. First off, each block contains not just the transaction data but also a cryptographic hash of the previous block. Think of it as a digital fingerprint that's unique to every block. Change one block, and you'd have to change the hashes for every block that follows, alerting the network to potential foul play.

Second, remember the decentralized nature of the system? Yep, it's a security feature too. An attacker would need to control more than 50% of the nodes to make any changes, which is logistically and financially ludicrous. This makes blockchain one of the safest ways to record transactions or any digital interaction for that matter.

Potential Applications Beyond Bitcoin

As we wrap up this chapter, let's venture beyond Bitcoin. The applications of blockchain technology are as limitless as the cosmos. Imagine voting systems where every vote is transparent yet anonymous. Envision healthcare records that are secure, easily accessible, and tamper-proof. What about supply chains that are traceable, from farm to table?

Smart contracts, digital IDs, peer-to-peer networks—the potential is staggering. Blockchain could revolutionize not just how we deal with money, but how we interact, govern, and even live. It's not just a game-changer; it's a world-changer.

Phew! That was a lot, but you made it through, and now you're that much wiser. You can now explain blockchain technology to anyone who'll listen (or even those who won't).

So, you see, blockchain isn't just the backbone of Bitcoin; it's the future of decentralized, secure, and transparent systems. Your mind is probably racing with the possibilities, and rightly so. But hang on; we've still got more riveting chapters ahead!

Chapter 4:

The Psychology of Cryptocurrency: Why Bitcoin Matters

Ahoy, and welcome back! By now, you're a little more blockchain-savvy, you understand the basics of Bitcoin, and maybe you've even dabbled in a transaction or two. But have you ever stopped to think about what's going on in that noggin of yours and the collective minds of the Bitcoin universe? No worries if you haven't; that's what Chapter 4 is all about!

Emotional Factors Driving Bitcoin Adoption

Let's start with the feels. Why do people get into Bitcoin in the first place? Well, there's the obvious FOMO (Fear of Missing Out). Who hasn't heard tales of people becoming overnight millionaires because they hopped on the Bitcoin wagon early? There's something deeply enticing about the idea of snagging a part of the future before everyone else catches on. And let's not forget the adrenaline rush of seeing Bitcoin's value skyrocket, even if it also plummets the next day.

But it's not just about money. Many see Bitcoin as a way to break free from the shackles of traditional banking systems and governmental control. It's not just a currency; it's a revolution! An emotional investment in freedom, if you will.

Cognitive Biases Affecting Trading and Investing

Let's put on our psychology hats for a minute. Ever heard of confirmation bias? It's that nifty little trick your brain does where it pays more attention to information that confirms your existing beliefs. In the world of Bitcoin, this can mean overly focusing on success stories while ignoring cautionary tales.

Another classic is the anchoring effect, where people fixate on specific prices, like buying Bitcoin only when it drops to a certain amount. Often, this means missing out on good opportunities or, worse, waiting for a dip that never comes.

The Community and Culture Around Bitcoin

Now, what's Bitcoin without its loyal fans, the Bitcoiners? This community isn't just about investing; it's a subculture with its own set of norms, jargon, and even memes. You're as likely to find discussions about philosophy and politics as you are about hash rates and market trends. It's like a digital Woodstock, but instead of flower crowns, there are cryptographic keys.

Behavioral Economics and Bitcoin

Here's where psychology meets wallet. Behavioral economics studies how emotional and psychological factors affect economic decisions. When it comes to Bitcoin, this can look like emotional trading, where the highs and lows of the market ride parallel to the rollercoaster of your emotions. Or the herd mentality, where people buy or sell based on what everyone else is doing, instead of careful analysis.

And then there's loss aversion. People generally hate losing more than they enjoy winning. This can lead to panicked selling at the first sign of a price dip, which only serves to destabilize the market further.

The Psychology of Bitcoin Skepticism

Now, we can't talk about the psychology of Bitcoin without mentioning its skeptics. You know the type—the ones who say it's all a bubble, a scam, or 'not real money.' At the core, this skepticism often stems from a lack of understanding or an attachment to traditional financial systems. But sometimes it's also a psychological defense mechanism against the fear of change or the unknown.

So, there you have it, a whirlwind tour of the human mind in the age of Bitcoin. It's a brave new world, filled with promise and pitfalls, guided not just by algorithms but also by our very human hopes, fears, and biases.

But don't take my word for it; dive into the community, do your research, and most importantly, understand your motivations and emotional drivers.

Like any frontier, the world of Bitcoin offers opportunities for glory but also chances for folly. The key to navigating it wisely lies not just in technical know-how but in understanding the psychological forces at play.

We've talked a lot, but there's still so much more to explore. Ready for the next chapter? It's going to be a page-turner!

Onward, my financially savvy friend! The next chapter promises more eye-openers and maybe, just maybe, will set you on the path to becoming a Bitcoin psychology guru!

(Disclaimer: This chapter doesn't substitute for professional financial or psychological advice. Always consult with experts before making significant financial decisions.)

And with that, let's move on to the next mind-bending chapter. Are you ready? Turn that page or swipe ahead; our Bitcoin adventure continues!

Chapter 5:

Setting Up Your Bitcoin Wallet: Your First Steps

Welcome back, intrepid future Bitcoin millionaire! Now that we've navigated the psychological landscape and peered into the blockchain's soul, it's time to get practical. After all, if Bitcoin were a treasure chest, a digital wallet would be your personal key. So buckle up as we delve into the nitty-gritty of setting up your Bitcoin wallet.

Types of Bitcoin Wallets Available

Picture this: wallets as a wardrobe. Some are the sweatpants of the Bitcoin world—comfortable and easy to use but maybe not the best for a high-stakes meeting. Others are the tuxedos—more complex, but oh-so secure. There are even wallet "accessories" that add an extra layer of flair (read: security).

Hot Wallets: These are your everyday, easy-to-access wallets that are connected to the internet. Great for quick transactions but not the safest place to store your life savings.

Cold Wallets: These are your safety deposit boxes—offline and secure. They're a little more cumbersome to access, but that's the point.

Hardware Wallets: Think of this as the Fort Knox of Bitcoin storage. These physical devices store your private keys offline.

Mobile Wallets: These are literally in your pocket at all times. Super convenient, but don't lose that phone!

Desktop Wallets: These reside on your personal computer. Great for those who prefer a bigger screen but remember, they can be vulnerable to malware.

How to Set Up a Wallet

Setting up a wallet can be as easy as downloading an app or as complex as constructing a maze for a secret treasure. Here's a simplified roadmap:

Choose Your Type: Decide on the kind of wallet that suits your needs.

Download or Purchase: Either download the software or buy the hardware.

Follow the Prompts: Most wallets come with setup instructions. Yes, it's that part of the assembly where you actually read the manual.

Generate Keys: Your wallet will automatically create a public address and a private key. Think of them as your email address and password, but for money.

Test It Out: Send a small amount of Bitcoin to your new address. Wait for it to show up in your wallet to make sure everything's working.

Best Practices for Wallet Security

Securing your wallet should be your numero uno priority. Think about it: you wouldn't leave your real wallet hanging around in a public place, right?

Two-Factor Authentication (2FA): This is like having a secret handshake with your wallet. An extra step, but worth it.

Regular Updates: Just like you wouldn't wear flared jeans from the 90s, you shouldn't have an outdated wallet. Keep that software fresh!

Backup: Save a copy of your wallet's essential info in another secure place. Physical copies are good; multiple secure digital copies are even better.

Be Phish-Proof: Watch out for suspicious emails or websites asking for your credentials. Even the most secure wallet can't protect you from your own mistakes.

Keep It Private: Your private key is like your toothbrush—no sharing!

The Importance of Backup and Recovery Phrases

"Be Prepared" isn't just the Scouts' motto; it should be yours too when it comes to your wallet. A backup is like a lifeboat for your digital assets. And your recovery phrase? That's the GPS to locate the lifeboat. Write it down, store it in a safe place, and whatever you do, don't forget where that is!

Mobile vs. Hardware vs Online Wallets

Let's break it down:

Mobile Wallets: Best for the on-the-go traders. Just don't lose your phone or step into a phishing trap.

Hardware Wallets: For those serious about security. Great for long-term storage, but don't forget where you stored the actual hardware!

Online Wallets: Easiest to set up and use, but just know you're entrusting your keys to a third party.

Phew, that was a lot! But you're now well-equipped to make your first foray into the Bitcoin world with your shiny new wallet.

So, all set to make that first Bitcoin purchase? You're on the threshold of a financial journey that's as exciting as it is revolutionary!

Just remember: the digital frontier is an ever-changing landscape. Keep updating, keep learning, and keep that wallet secure!

Go ahead and set up that wallet, because in the next chapter, we're diving deeper into the trading waters. How exciting is that?

Catch you in the next chapter, where we demystify the enigmatic world of Bitcoin exchanges. Until then, happy wallet-setting!

(Disclaimer: This chapter is not a substitute for professional financial advice. Always consult experts when making significant financial decisions.)

Onward to Chapter 6! Let's keep this crypto party going!

Chapter 6:

Understanding Bitcoin Exchanges: Where to Buy and Sell

Hey there, crypto-crusader! You've got your digital wallet all set up and are probably itching to dive into the bustling Bitcoin bazaar. But where does one actually go to buy and sell this digital gold? Welcome to the big league, pal—Bitcoin Exchanges!

Popular Bitcoin Exchanges

Let's kick it off with some heavy hitters in the Bitcoin trading arena:

Coinbase: The Coca-Cola of crypto exchanges. It's user-friendly and perfect for beginners.

Binance: A smorgasbord of cryptocurrencies to buy, sell, and swap. It's the international food court of digital currencies.

Kraken: The sea monster of crypto, known for its security features.

Bitstamp: One of the oldest in the game, it's like the wise old man of crypto exchanges.

Gemini: Think of it as the 'zodiac of security,' founded by the Winklevoss twins. Yes, those Winklevoss twins.

How to Choose an Exchange

Choosing an exchange is a bit like dating—you've got to find the right match. Here's what to look for:

Security: Ensure they have top-notch security features, like two-factor authentication.

User Experience: The interface should be as friendly as your grandma offering you cookies.

Transaction Fees: Nobody likes hidden fees, not even in the world of digital assets.

Variety of Coins: More coins mean more trading fun, right?

Customer Service: You want an exchange that answers faster than a teenager texting.

Setting Up and Securing Your Account

So, you've picked your exchange soulmate. What's next?

Account Creation: Usually as simple as entering your email and choosing a strong password. And no, 'password1234' doesn't count as strong.

Verification: For most exchanges, you'll need to prove you're not a robot or a dog on the internet. Usually involves some form of ID and possibly a selfie. No duck faces, please.

Security Features: Enable two-factor authentication, biometric logins, or whatever fancy features are offered. This is your Fort Knox, remember?

Initial Deposit: Time to put some money into this trading adventure. This is like buying chips at a casino, only less risky (if done right).

Test Drive: Many exchanges have a 'demo' feature. Think of this as your training wheels.

Buying and Selling Strategies

Ah, strategy—the chess game of trading. Whether you're a day trader or a long-term investor, it's essential to have a game plan.

Know Your Budget: Only invest what you can afford to lose. Seriously.

Market Research: There are a plethora of tools out there to help you read the market. They're like the CliffsNotes for trading.

Buy Low, Sell High: Easier said than done, but that's basically the gist of it.

Dollar-Cost Averaging (DCA): This strategy involves buying a fixed dollar amount of Bitcoin at regular intervals, regardless of its price. It's like the crockpot of investment strategies—set it and forget it.

Take Profits and Cut Losses: Know when to hold 'em and when to fold 'em, as the song goes.

Withdrawal and Deposit Methods

This is the nuts and bolts—how you get your money in and out of the exchange:

Bank Transfers: Slow but steady. Your grandma's method, but it works.

Credit/Debit Cards: Fast, but watch for fees that can eat into your budget like a kid in a candy store.

Crypto Transfers: Move your Bitcoin from one wallet to another. It's the "beaming up" of the crypto world.

PayPal and Other E-services: Fast and convenient but do check if the exchange supports it.

ATMs: Yes, there are Bitcoin ATMs. No, they don't dispense physical Bitcoins. That would be cool though, wouldn't it?

Well, that wraps up our whirlwind tour of Bitcoin Exchanges!

Remember, trading Bitcoin isn't just about making quick bucks; it's a long-term commitment.

So there you have it, you're now ready to make some educated decisions on where to trade your hard-earned money for some hard-coded Bitcoin.

See you in the next chapter, where we'll look into basic trading techniques. May the coins be ever in your favor!

(Disclaimer: This chapter is not a substitute for professional financial advice. Always consult experts when making significant financial decisions.)

Off we go, onto Chapter 7! The journey to Bitcoin Millionaire status continues!

(Note: Always do your own due diligence and consult financial advisors before making any investment decisions.)

Chapter 7:

Basic Trading Techniques: Tips and Strategies for Beginners

Ah, trading! That exhilarating world where people in suits shout, throw papers in the air, and bang on desks. Wait, that's the movies; let's talk about real-life trading, where most of the drama happens right in your comfy pajamas while you're sipping on some coffee.

First thing's first, let's get chummy with some basic trading lingo. Picture yourself in a new country; you'd need to learn the local language to get by, right? Similarly, in the world of Bitcoin trading, terms like "bullish," "bearish," "long," and "short" aren't referring to moods or dimensions, but rather market trends and positions. If you hear someone saying they're "bullish," it means they expect the price to rise, and if they're "bearish," well, they're preparing for a downturn. "Going long" is essentially buying with the expectation that the value will increase, and "going short" is the complete opposite—you sell, anticipating the price will drop.

Now, don't let the term "reading Bitcoin charts" intimidate you. It's like reading a comic book, but instead of Batman fighting the Joker, it's you combating volatility. The most common one you'll encounter is a "candlestick chart." Each candlestick represents a specific timeframe, and its color indicates whether the price went up or down. The "wick" of the candlestick shows the price range, from the highest to the lowest during that period. A lot easier than interpreting ancient hieroglyphs, right?

Let's now shift gears to the different types of orders you can place. You've got market, limit, and stop orders—no, these aren't coffee choices at Starbucks but methods to control your trading activities. A "market order" is like ordering fast food; you get what's readily available. Your purchase or sale goes through immediately at the current market price. A "limit order," on the other hand, is more like a reservation at a fine dining restaurant. You specify the price at which you'd like to buy or sell, and the order only executes if that price is met. Finally, a "stop order" is your financial safety net. It only becomes active once a predetermined price is reached, and then it behaves like a market order. Consider it the "break glass in case of emergency" option of trading.

Risk management isn't just for tightrope walkers and lion tamers; it's crucial for traders, too. After all, it's your hard-earned money that's on the line. One useful tip is the "1% rule," where you never risk more than 1% of your total trading capital on a single trade. This allows you to live to trade another day, even if things don't go your way. Diversification is another method to mitigate risks; it's like not putting all your eggs in one basket, or in this case, not putting all your Bitcoins in one wallet. Make sure you also keep an eye on external factors like news events, regulatory changes, and macroeconomic indicators, as they can have a massive impact on Bitcoin's price. In essence, think of risk management as your protective helmet in the trading arena.

Profit-taking and loss-cutting are as vital as scoring goals and defending them in a soccer match. The objective is simple: maximize gains and minimize losses. If a trade is going well, don't let greed cloud your judgment; it's perfectly acceptable to take profits off the table. On the flip side, if a trade is spiraling downwards faster than a roller coaster, it's wise to cut your losses. One popular strategy is setting a "take profit" or "stop loss" level, where your position automatically closes once it hits a certain price. It's like having a personal assistant who's solely focused on preserving your wealth.

Well, look at you, making it through an entire chapter on trading techniques! You're now ready to dip your toes in the Bitcoin trading pool. Sure, the water might be a bit chilly at first, but as you get the hang of it, you'll find it's not just bearable, it's exhilarating. The important thing is to start slow, learn continuously, and always stay disciplined. You didn't learn to ride a bike in a day, and you won't become a trading pro overnight, either.

So, go ahead, open that trading app, take a deep breath, and place your first order. After all, every Bitcoin millionaire started with a single trade. On to the next chapter, where we're scaling up the trading ladder to advanced techniques. Ready to level up? The game is afoot!

Chapter 8:

Advanced Trading Techniques: Taking Your Portfolio to New Heights

Welcome back, trading aficionado! Feeling good about the basics? Fantastic! You've got your trading seatbelt fastened, and now it's time to put this vehicle into fifth gear and explore the autobahn of advanced trading. Buckle up because things are about to get turbocharged!

First up in our pit stop of advanced techniques is leverage and margin trading. Imagine for a moment that you're a superhero, and leverage is your superpower. It gives you the ability to amplify your strength (capital in this case) to perform heroic acts (trades, obviously). But remember, with great power comes great responsibility! Leverage allows you to trade with more money than you actually have in your account. You're essentially borrowing money to maximize your profits. But beware, because losses can also be amplified, and nobody wants to be the superhero who ends up tearing their cape. You need to be like Spider-Man: agile and aware of your surroundings, always ready to swing away from impending danger.

Now let's talk about shorting Bitcoin. No, it's not the act of making Bitcoin smaller, though wouldn't that be neat? Shorting is betting that the price of Bitcoin will fall. This may seem counterintuitive when everyone around you is championing for Bitcoin to reach for the stars. But markets have ups and downs; they breathe in and out like a living organism. When you short Bitcoin, you sell it at a higher price with the intention of buying it back when the price drops. You get to pocket the difference, essentially profiting from the market's misfortune. It's like finding a twenty-dollar bill on the ground; it might not be ideal for the person who lost it, but hey, you're not complaining.

On to the futuristic world of algorithmic trading! If traditional trading is like playing chess, then algorithmic trading is like having a supercomputer calculate your every move. This method uses computer programs to automate trading decisions based on certain criteria. Want to buy when the price hits a certain level? There's an algorithm for that. Want to sell when the price starts to dip after reaching an all-time high? Yep, there's an algorithm for that too. The computer does the heavy lifting, leaving you free to sip your mojito and work on that novel you've always wanted to write. But remember, even supercomputers can crash, so it's crucial to have a backup strategy in case things go haywire.

Ah, advanced technical analysis—the Da Vinci Code of trading. This is where you look at price charts and see not just lines and numbers, but also patterns, trends, and indicators. You're basically the Sherlock Holmes of the trading world, deciphering clues and making deductions. Head and Shoulders, Double Tops, Bollinger Bands—these aren't just random phrases but valuable tools in your investigative kit. Advanced technical analysis helps you forecast future price movements with greater accuracy.

It's like being able to predict the weather and knowing exactly when to carry an umbrella.

Finally, let's talk about something people usually avoid discussing at dinner parties—taxes. Trading Bitcoin isn't a tax-free amusement park ride; there are ticket fees involved. When you make profits from trading, Uncle Sam wants his share. The specifics vary by jurisdiction, but short-term and long-term capital gains are the most common categories. Keeping a meticulous record of all your transactions can be a lifesaver come tax season. You don't want to be digging through a year's worth of email receipts two days before the deadline, trust me.

Well, there you have it—the Swiss Army knife of advanced trading techniques. You're no longer just a player; you're a pro in the making. These skills won't just take your portfolio to new heights; they'll launch it into a different stratosphere. Now, you're not just surviving the trading jungle; you're dominating it. Ready to unleash these advanced techniques on the unsuspecting world? Your trading app is beckoning you. So go on, tap into that inner Maverick and take your portfolio to the moon and beyond!

Chapter 9:

Security Measures: Protecting Your Digital Wealth

Ahoy, matey! Welcome aboard the S.S. Security, where we sail the turbulent seas of the digital world. We're on a quest to guard our treasure—our oh-so-precious Bitcoin—and I'm Captain Safety, your trusty guide. Arrr you ready to set sail? Let's embark on an adventure that'll make Blackbeard jealous of our impenetrable vaults!

So, you've amassed your Bitcoin treasure, and it's shining brighter than a Caribbean sunset. But what's that? Pirates are on the horizon! Digital pirates, that is. Cybersecurity is the modern-day pirate warfare, and our first line of defense is Two-Factor Authentication, or 2FA as it's known among the tech-savvy parrots. Think of 2FA as the padlock on your treasure chest. Even if someone steals the key (your password), they can't open it without the secret combination (a code sent to your phone, for example). It's like having a guard dog that only listens to your voice. Ah, the wonders of modern technology!

Now let's talk about cold storage solutions, which is the equivalent of hiding your treasure chest in an underwater cave guarded by mermaids and sea monsters. In the world of Bitcoin, cold storage means keeping your coins offline, far away from the prying eyes of the internet. Imagine your Bitcoin as golden doubloons. You wouldn't just leave them sitting on the deck of your ship, would you? No, you'd bury them deep, mark it on a secret map, and maybe even set some booby traps for good measure. Cold storage is your digital "X marks the spot," where your wealth is securely tucked away.

But wait, the waters are getting rougher! Phishing attempts are like sirens of the sea, trying to lure you into their deceitful traps. These scams usually arrive in the form of emails or messages that look legitimate but are as fake as a three-legged pirate claiming to be a ballet dancer. They'll try to trick you into revealing your personal information, singing a sweet song of "urgent account issues" or "congratulations, you've won!" Don't listen! Block your ears and sail away, because once they have your info, they'll raid your digital ship faster than you can say "Shiver me timbers!"

What's that in your hand, sailor? A hardware wallet? You savvy sea dog, you! Hardware wallets are like portable treasure chests that you can carry around, and they're nigh impossible to break into. It's a piece of hardware that stores your Bitcoin keys offline. If cold storage is the hidden cave for your treasure, then a hardware wallet is the sturdy, unbreakable chest inside that cave. Plus, it's a lot easier to carry around than a massive chest of gold.

And last but not least, let's discuss VPNs and secure connections, the magical cloaks of invisibility in our maritime metaphor. VPN stands for Virtual Private Network, and it disguises your online activity as if you were sailing under a pirate flag. It's the perfect tool for when you're docking in uncharted ports (public Wi-Fi) where local brigands (hackers) are known to lurk. With a VPN, you can make transactions and browse the web without leaving a trail of breadcrumbs for scallywags to follow.

Phew! We've weathered some serious storms, but we've come out unscathed with our treasure intact. We've talked about 2FA, the padlock for your digital wealth; delved into cold storage, the secret cavern for your treasure; learned how to spot phishing attempts, the sirens of the online world; embraced hardware wallets, the unbreakable chests of crypto; and sailed securely with VPNs, our digital pirate flags.

So there you have it—a treasure map for navigating the perilous waters of digital security. Keep your cutlass sharp and your wits sharper, because in the world of Bitcoin, the adventure never ends. The horizon is filled with possibilities and dangers alike, but now you're well-equipped to face whatever lies ahead.

Fair winds and following seas, crypto pirate! Your treasure is now as secure as Fort Knox, and the digital high seas have never seen a pirate as savvy as you. So go on, hoist the Jolly Roger of security and set sail for new crypto adventures. Your treasure isn't just safe; it's Fort Knox in a pirate ship!

And remember, in the words of a famous sea shanty: "Heave ho, thieves and beggars, never shall we die!" Especially not in the treacherous seas of the digital age, where you're now the most secure swashbuckler around! Yarrrr!

Chapter 10:

Tax Implications: Navigating the Legal Landscape

Welcome to the maze, the labyrinth, the enigma wrapped in a conundrum that is cryptocurrency taxation! Think of it as that mysterious level in a video game where you're navigating through traps and collecting golden coins—only these coins aren't just digital tokens; they're real, actual money that can buy you a speedboat or a tropical island. Okay, maybe not a whole island, but you get the idea. And just like in a game, there are rules you need to play by if you don't want to get a "Game Over" from the Taxman Boss Level.

Firstly, let's talk about the basics of cryptocurrency taxation. Uncle Sam is quite interested in your digital treasure chest. You see, to the IRS, cryptocurrency is property, not currency, which is sort of like saying a tomato is a fruit, not a vegetable—it changes how you make your salad. What this means is that you're subject to capital gains tax whenever you sell or trade your cryptocurrency. Think of it as your share of the pirate booty that you have to give to the governing island; otherwise, you'll end up walking the plank—or in our case, dealing with fines and audits.

Now, onto record-keeping for transactions. This is the unsexy but crucial part of being a crypto adventurer. Picture it as the logbook you keep on your pirate ship, jotting down every treasure you loot and every bottle of rum you buy. You'll want to record the date of each transaction, the amount, what it was for, and the value in U.S. dollars at the time of the transaction. Imagine explaining to an angry kraken why you shouldn't be its dinner—that's how detailed your records should be to explain to the IRS if they ever come knocking.

Let's talk about taxable events, shall we? These are the 'Eureka!' moments in your crypto journey. Every time you sell your crypto for fiat currency (that's regular money, like dollars or euros), trade one cryptocurrency for another, or make a purchase using your crypto, you trigger a taxable event. It's like setting off a firework that alerts the IRS ship to your location. Remember that even swapping your shiny Bitcoin for another cryptocurrency is considered a sale and, thus, a taxable event. And let's not forget about crypto you earn through mining or get as payment for services; the IRS wants a piece of that pie too.

Alright, on to legal considerations and potential pitfalls. As you swashbuckle your way through the crypto seas, keep in mind that tax laws can be as unpredictable as a rogue wave. There are regulatory shifts, changing tax rates, and evolving definitions of what constitutes a taxable event. So, keep an eye on the horizon for changes that could affect your treasure. Be cautious, for there be legal dragons here; misreporting your taxes can lead to penalties, and tax evasion is as frowned upon in the crypto world as it is in any other realm.

Finally, a pirate is only as good as their crew, and when it comes to taxes, your best mateys are certified tax professionals with experience in cryptocurrency. Sure, doing it alone is possible, but consulting an expert is like having a seasoned navigator aboard, steering you clear of treacherous waters. Don't be that stubborn pirate who sails into a storm shouting, "I know what I'm doing!" You might not, and it's okay to ask for help.

There we have it, fellow adventurers, a whirlwind tour through the dizzying labyrinth of cryptocurrency taxation. It might seem like a daunting level, but with your logbook in hand and a savvy tax professional by your side, you'll be well-equipped to sail through with your treasure intact.

So, what's next on our quest? Will we find the fabled island of Tax-Free Gains? Probably not, but we'll be well-prepared for anything the Taxman Boss Level throws our way. And remember, knowing is half the battle—the other half is not getting audited. So, hoist the anchor, set the sails, and let's navigate through this sea of codes and regulations like the crypto pirates we are!

May your gains be high, your taxes low, and your navigation through the legal maze smoother than a calm sea at dawn! Ahoy!

Chapter 11:

Bitcoin Mining: The Backbone of the Network

Welcome to the mystical world of Bitcoin mining, where you're part modern-day alchemist, part tech wizard. You're probably wondering, "What in the blockchain is Bitcoin mining?" No, it doesn't involve pickaxes or underground tunnels. Mining in the Bitcoin universe is the computational process that validates transactions on the Bitcoin network and adds them to the public ledger, known as the blockchain. It's like being the ultimate hall monitor, except instead of a shiny badge, you get shiny new Bitcoins.

Bitcoin mining is essential because it contributes to the security and stability of the network. Think of it as the gears and cogs behind the gilded Bitcoin clock face. Miners, with their computational power, solve complex mathematical problems. The first to solve it gets to add a new block to the blockchain and is rewarded with newly minted Bitcoin and transaction fees. So, you're not only the hall monitor but also the quiz champion of the cyberworld!

Ah, but setting up a mining operation isn't just a walk in the park. It's more like setting up a space station on a distant planet, metaphorically speaking. First, you need the right hardware. In the early days of Bitcoin, you could mine using your personal computer. Those were the days! Now you need specialized mining hardware known as

ASICs (Application-Specific Integrated Circuits), which are tailored to efficiently perform the Bitcoin hashing function. This isn't cheap equipment, so think of it as an investment, like buying a top-of-the-line fishing rod when you're really into angling.

Of course, having a powerful machine alone won't make you a Bitcoin billionaire. You need to join forces with other miners in a "mining pool." This is like forming a superhero team where each member contributes their unique power—in this case, computational power—to solve problems faster. Pooling resources means that you're more likely to solve a problem quickly and earn that sweet, sweet Bitcoin. However, remember that you'll be sharing the loot based on the amount of work each member contributed. But hey, a slice of the Bitcoin pie is better than no pie at all, right?

And let's not forget the cost of energy. These mining machines eat electricity for breakfast, lunch, and dinner. To maximize profitability, many miners seek locations where electricity is cheap. Some even set up near renewable energy sources to lower costs and appeal to the eco-conscious. So, if you're thinking of hosting a mining rig, consider the electric bill and maybe even consult an electrician. You don't want to trip the whole neighborhood's power supply!

Ah yes, let's talk numbers, shall we? Economic viability is a significant concern. Sure, you can technically mine Bitcoin with your laptop, but you'd spend more on electricity than you'd make in Bitcoin. The key to successful mining is optimizing your operation's scale and efficiency. Keep an eye on the Bitcoin market and consider setting stop-losses or automated systems to sell Bitcoin during high price peaks. Yes, you've got to strategize like a general leading troops into financial battle.

The act of mining itself is a fascinating interplay of probabilities and luck. Each miner or mining pool is in a race to solve the next block. The more computational power you have, the higher your chances, but it's not a guarantee. It's like being in a high-stakes lottery where the jackpot is a bunch of Bitcoin.

Bitcoin mining may seem like it's all about the individual, but it's also a community endeavor. Miners often communicate and collaborate, sharing best practices, pooling resources, and discussing trends. There's even a term for when miners collectively agree to update protocols— a "consensus." Achieving consensus is like getting all your friends to agree on where to go for dinner, only way more complex and with much higher stakes.

Finally, remember that Bitcoin mining is not a get-rich-quick scheme. It's a venture that requires careful planning, investment, and a bit of luck. You need to consider hardware costs, electricity expenses, and the potential returns. Always do your own research (commonly abbreviated as DYOR in the crypto-sphere), and maybe even consult with financial advisors who understand the nuances of crypto.

In summary, if you decide to go down this mining rabbit hole, you'll be part of a community that's at the forefront of financial and technological innovation. You'll contribute to the stability of a revolutionary system and, if you're lucky and strategic, you could earn a handsome reward for your efforts.

So, are you ready to join the mining revolution? Strap on your virtual hard hat and get ready to dig into the digital earth. The blockchain awaits your contribution!

Chapter 12:

Altcoins and Tokens:

The Extended Cryptocurrency Universe

Welcome to Chapter 12, where we venture beyond the Bitcoin galaxy and into the wider universe of altcoins and tokens! Imagine if Bitcoin were a Hollywood blockbuster—well, altcoins are the indie films and foreign language cinema of the crypto world. Not as mainstream, maybe, but some are just as compelling and potentially even more rewarding.

Altcoins, short for "alternative coins," are exactly what the name implies: alternatives to Bitcoin. While Bitcoin is the granddaddy of them all, think of altcoins as its energetic, sometimes quirky, often brilliant grandchildren. Each has its own unique features, benefits, and yes, drawbacks. From Ethereum's smart contracts to Ripple's banking solutions, each altcoin offers a different approach to decentralized assets.

If you're a crypto-curious explorer, you might want to venture into the lands of popular altcoins like Ethereum, Litecoin, or Cardano. Ethereum, for example, isn't just a cryptocurrency; it's a whole platform that enables smart contracts and builds decentralized applications. Imagine creating a self-executing contract that doesn't need a middleman, like an unstoppable vending machine that's also a lawyer!

Then there's the fascinating world of tokens. Wait, tokens and coins are different? Absolutely! Think of it like this: if altcoins are foreign films, tokens are like the film festival passes that let you experience various screenings. Coins like Bitcoin or Litecoin exist on their own blockchains, whereas tokens are built on top of another blockchain, like Ethereum. Tokens often represent assets or utilities and can be used in multiple ways within their native ecosystem. Ever heard of NFTs or Non-Fungible Tokens? They're like the collectible action figures of the digital world, each with its unique characteristics, all enabled by token technology.

Now, let's talk trading and investing in altcoins. You already learned the ropes with Bitcoin, and the mechanics of trading altcoins are generally the same. However, the volatility game is on a whole new level. Altcoins can experience even wilder price swings, turning you into either a genius investor or someone with a lot of explaining to do at the next family gathering. So, while there's a lot of money to be made, there's also a considerable amount of risk involved. Think of it as the crypto version of skydiving: exhilarating but not for the faint of heart.

Here's the tricky part—altcoins are often less liquid than Bitcoin. That means fewer buyers and sellers, which can result in more dramatic price changes. The flip side? It also means opportunity. Some investors have found significant rewards in 'low-cap gems,' smaller, less known coins with the potential for huge returns. It's like discovering an underground band before they hit it big; you could be the one who says, "I knew them when."

Ah, but don't get swept away by the siren song of these alternative cryptocurrencies without considering the risks. Scams and pump-and-dump schemes are more common in the world of altcoins. Plus, the lack of regulation and oversight means you're really out in the wild west of finance. You should, therefore, tread carefully, do extensive research, and maybe don't put all your eggs—or coins—in one basket.

In summary, the universe of altcoins and tokens is as diverse and complex as a coral reef. Some are beautiful, some have the potential to sting, but all are fascinating to explore. They provide not only investment opportunities but also a chance to support technologies and communities that could revolutionize various aspects of our lives.

So, if you're ready to expand your crypto horizons, consider dipping your toes into the captivating waters of altcoins and tokens. Just remember your digital snorkel and safety gear (read: solid research and risk assessment) as you explore these colorful depths. Happy diving!

Chapter 13:

Bitcoin in Business: Revolutionizing Commerce

So, you've mastered the ins and outs of Bitcoin for personal use—bravo! But hold your horses, the Bitcoin rollercoaster doesn't stop there. In fact, it has extended its tracks into the realm of business, stirring the pot and cooking up some real change in the commercial world. Yeah, Bitcoin isn't just for buying a cup of coffee or nabbing some cool online merchandise anymore. Businesses are getting in on the action, and it's about time we chat about it.

Using Bitcoin for Payments and Transactions

Ah, the cash register, an iconic symbol of brick-and-mortar commerce for decades. But let's be real, paper money and coins are so last century. Enter Bitcoin, a new-age hero swooping in to simplify transactions and cut down on those pesky fees. Whether it's a giant corporation or a small mom-and-pop shop, Bitcoin's ease of use and low transaction costs are making it an attractive option for business owners worldwide.

Now, while it's cool to daydream about a world where you can pay for everything with Bitcoin, from your morning latte to your car service, we're not quite there yet. But the movement is growing, and it's growing fast. Several online platforms have made it a breeze for businesses to integrate Bitcoin payments, and even some physical stores are displaying those stylish "Bitcoin Accepted Here" signs.

Smart Contracts and Their Applications

Imagine sealing a deal without the need for lengthy legal documents or third-party intermediaries. That's the magic of smart contracts. Basically, they're self-executing contracts with the terms directly coded into lines of software. This ensures both parties hold up their end of the bargain without any fuss.

Smart contracts are especially making waves in the real estate and entertainment industries. For example, an artist could set up a smart contract to automatically receive royalties every time their song is streamed. No middlemen, no waiting, and certainly no dodgy business.

Supply Chain Management with Blockchain

Oh, the supply chain—where products journey from factories to shelves, crossing borders, time zones, and sometimes even ethical boundaries. But what if we could make that process more transparent and efficient? Bitcoin's underlying technology, blockchain, is here to save the day.

From the moment an item is produced to the second it lands in a consumer's hands, every step can be recorded on a blockchain. This eliminates the fog of uncertainty that often shrouds the supply chain, making it transparent, traceable, and a whole lot more trustworthy.

Bitcoin's Role in International Trade

The global marketplace is like a never-ending game of Monopoly, but with more rules, regulations, and well, actual stakes. Traditional currencies have long been the default medium of trade, but they come with their own set of challenges—like exchange rates, fees, and time delays. Bitcoin sidesteps these issues, offering a uniform currency that can be used from Timbuktu to Tokyo without missing a beat.

Regulatory Challenges for Businesses

So far, so good, right? But hold on, not everything is as rosy as it seems. The fast-paced adoption of Bitcoin in business has also caught the eyes of regulators. While some countries are embracing it, others are laying down the law, setting up rules and regulations that businesses must adhere to. Compliance is key, and let's face it, the rules of the game are still being written.

Chapter 14:

Investing Long-Term: Hodling Strategies

Ah, the word "HODL." If you've been around the crypto block—even just a little—you've surely stumbled upon this curious term that's become the rallying cry for an entire community of long-term believers. It's more than just a misspelled word; it's an ethos, a lifestyle, and for some, a pretty sound financial strategy.

The Philosophy Behind "HODLing

Let's kick things off by clearing the air. HODL is not some highfalutin acronym that stands for a complex investment formula. Nope, it's far more poetic than that. A typo made by a user in a crypto forum has now snowballed into a whole investment philosophy. In essence, "HODLing" is the art of holding on to your crypto investments through the ups and downs, the highs and lows, and whatever market tantrums come your way. And why do people HODL? Because they believe in the long-term value of cryptocurrencies, Bitcoin or otherwise. It's the financial equivalent of "in sickness and in health."

Long-term vs Short-Term Investments

Now, not to disparage the day traders out there who live for the thrills and spills of short-term plays. But HODLing is like the comfort food of crypto investment—satisfying and dependable. When you're aiming for long-term gains, you're less concerned about the daily volatility and more focused on the bigger picture. It's less about timing the market and more about time in the market.

Short-term investments may offer immediate gratification, but they're also akin to a high-wire act without a safety net. Long-term HODLing, on the other hand, is more like planting a seed and patiently watering it, expecting a lush tree down the road.

Strategies for Diversifying Your Crypto Portfolio

Let's talk diversification, the buzzword that even your grandma might be throwing around these days. But it's popular for a reason; spreading your investments across different assets can safeguard you against unforeseen calamities. In the crypto world, this means not putting all your digital eggs in one basket. Sure, Bitcoin is the Beyoncé of cryptocurrencies, but there are plenty of other talented altcoins out there deserving of your attention.

A diversified portfolio might include a mix of established coins like Bitcoin and Ethereum, along with some promising newcomers. You could also look into different sectors within the crypto space—like DeFi, NFTs, or supply chain tokens. The idea is to build a portfolio that can weather various storms, not just the occasional drizzle.

Passive Income Through Staking or Lending

While HODLing sounds passive, it doesn't mean you can't make your crypto work for you. Enter staking and lending, the set-it-and-forget-it slow cookers of the crypto world. Staking allows you to lock up a portion of your coins to help validate transactions and secure the network. In return, you get additional coins as a reward. It's like getting paid in dividends but in a far cooler, more futuristic way.

Lending your crypto is another avenue for generating passive income. Through decentralized platforms, you can lend your coins to other users and earn interest over time. It's essentially playing the bank but without the drab suits and long lines.

Evaluating Market Cycles for Long-Term Investment

Ah, the market cycle, the great wheel of fortune that can make or break your investment dreams. While it's impossible to predict every twist and turn, understanding the basic stages—optimism, belief, euphoria, and the inevitable downturn—can help you gauge when to double down or, contrary to the HODL spirit, when to cut and run. Even long-term investments need occasional check-ins, like a plant that requires pruning or a pet that needs a vet visit.

In conclusion, HODLing is not just a meme or a catchy slogan; it's a viable long-term strategy that's garnered a loyal following for good reasons. The world of crypto is still young, vibrant, and full of potential. So why not grab a comfy seat, make some popcorn, and enjoy the long, exhilarating ride?

Chapter 15:

The Dark Side: Risks and Scams to Avoid

Ah, if only the world of cryptocurrency were all rainbows, unicorns, and exponential growth curves! But let's not kid ourselves; it's more like a thrilling roller coaster ride that occasionally goes through some spooky tunnels. Just like you wouldn't go on a space adventure without understanding the risks of, say, asteroid collisions or misplacing your helmet, diving into crypto also calls for a good awareness of the dark alleys you'd best steer clear of.

Common Scams in the Cryptocurrency World

Okay, first up: scams. Picture this—you're scrolling through social media, minding your own business, when you spot an ad promising astronomical returns on a new "can't-miss" crypto coin. The coin's name? "ToTheMoonARoo!" Sounds legit, right? Well, beware of too-good-to-be-true deals. They're the cryptocurrency world's version of the snake oil salesman. Pump-and-dump schemes, fake giveaways, and phishing scams are just a few of the traps laid by the not-so-nice people in the crypto neighborhood.

Red Flags to Watch For

Now, you might be wondering, "How do I spot these scammers?" Well, they usually come with a set of red flags—loud, blaring ones if you know what to look for. First, promises of guaranteed, sky-high returns are your first clue. Life gives no guarantees, my friend, and that especially applies to the volatile crypto market. Another red flag? Anonymity. If you can't find any information about the team behind the project, it's best to keep your crypto wallet firmly closed.

The Dark Web and Its Connection to Bitcoin

Alright, moving on to another shadowy subject: the dark web. You know, the part of the internet where your regular search engines fear to tread? While Bitcoin itself is not inherently nefarious, its pseudo-anonymous nature makes it a favored currency in these less-than-savory online corners. To be clear, the vast majority of Bitcoin transactions are above board and perfectly legal. However, just like you wouldn't want to be caught holding a bag of counterfeit money, it's important to know where your Bitcoin is coming from.

Regulatory Risks and Legal Challenges

Let's pivot a bit and talk about another type of risk—legal and regulatory. Imagine this: you've just settled down with a nice cup of tea, and boom—headlines scream that your country is considering banning cryptocurrencies. Regulatory news can send shockwaves through the market, affecting prices and potentially your investment. Governments are still figuring out how to approach this new technology, so be prepared for a ride through the legislative loop-de-loop.

Steps for Securing Your Investment

Now that we've scared you sufficiently, let's talk about how you can armor up and protect yourself. Basic measures like using two-factor authentication, keeping your crypto in a hardware wallet, and not clicking on suspicious links are like the seat belts and airbags of your crypto journey. Due diligence is another non-negotiable. This means thoroughly researching any investment opportunity and keeping abreast of news that could impact the market.

The wonderful thing about the crypto space is its dynamism and the potential for anyone and everyone to get involved. But this is a world where the phrase "knowledge is power" holds especially true. The more you know, the better equipped you'll be to navigate through both the sunlit uplands and the inevitable darker patches.

So, there you have it! While the crypto space has its share of risks and challenges, with a bit of caution and a good dose of common sense, you can steer clear of most pitfalls. Now, on to brighter topics in the next chapter, shall we?

Chapter 16:

Real-World Applications: Bitcoin Beyond Trading

So, you thought Bitcoin was all about amassing digital fortunes, lurking on exchanges, and feverishly checking price charts? Well, guess again! The magical world of Bitcoin and other cryptocurrencies extends far beyond the confines of trading screens. In fact, you'll find Bitcoin casually mingling in sectors you might never have imagined—kind of like that guy who shows up at every party but nobody knows how he got invited. Let's delve into some of the intriguing roles that Bitcoin has taken on outside the trading sphere.

Bitcoin in Remittances and Micropayments

Picture Maria, a hardworking mom who moved overseas to provide a better life for her family back home. Every month, she sends money back to her children. Traditional remittance services might gobble up a good chunk of that money in fees. But thanks to Bitcoin, Maria can transfer funds swiftly and at a fraction of the cost, maximizing the chicken nuggets and school supplies her kids can get. Pretty heartwarming, eh?

And then there's John, an avid blog reader who wants to tip his favorite writers. He doesn't want to commit to a subscription, but he's happy to pay a tiny amount for each article he enjoys. Enter Bitcoin micropayments, which allow him to send a handful of cents without incurring outrageous fees. It's like tossing a coin into a busker's hat but in digital form.

Blockchain for Social Impact

Alright, enough of money talk for a minute. Let's switch gears and think about doing good for society. Social impact projects are using blockchain to create transparent and tamper-proof systems for things like charitable donations and election voting. Now, every time you give to a cause, you could trace exactly where your contribution is going. Imagine a world where you know for sure that your donation to save the honeybees actually goes to the honeybees and not to pay for an NGO's office snacks. Sweet, right?

Bitcoin in the Arts and NFTs

Ah, art—the soul food that feeds our culture. You might be scratching your head, wondering what Bitcoin could possibly have to do with art. Well, a lot, actually! Non-fungible tokens, or NFTs, have blown the art world's roof off, allowing artists to tokenize their work and sell it digitally. So, next time you hear about a pixelated image selling for millions, don't scoff. That's an artist getting their due in the crypto world.

The Role of Bitcoin in Financial Inclusion

You've probably heard the term "financial inclusion" bandied about, but let's give it the stage for a moment. There are billions of people worldwide without access to traditional banking. Yes, you read that right—billions, with a "b." For these individuals, Bitcoin provides a lifeline to financial services through just a smartphone. It's like a financial Swiss Army knife, useful for various monetary needs, and all without the red tape and bureaucracy of conventional banks.

Crypto in the Gig Economy

Last but not least, let's talk about the gig economy—home to freelancers, side-hustlers, and everyone else who decided that a 9-to-5 just wasn't their cup of tea. Bitcoin and other cryptocurrencies are becoming increasingly popular as methods of payment for gigs. It's fast, it's international, and it avoids the pesky fees that usually accompany cross-border transactions. Plus, for many, the cool factor of being paid in crypto is a bonus that's hard to quantify but easy to appreciate.

So, let's zoom out and take in the big picture. Bitcoin isn't just an investment vehicle or a speculative tool. It's a multi-talented wonder, stretching its influence across sectors as diverse as charity, art, and even day-to-day chores like sending money to grandma. Whether you're an artist, a philanthropist, a freelancer, or just someone who likes to send a tip for a well-written blog post, Bitcoin has something for you.

Isn't it amazing how versatile this digital marvel is? It's not just shaking up the financial world; it's making waves in practically every aspect of our lives. I hope this chapter broadens your perspective on what Bitcoin can do and encourages you to explore these other avenues. Now, you'll have way more to talk about at dinner parties than just the latest price swings! Shall we move on to the next chapter?

Chapter 17:

Social and Cultural Impact: Changing the Global Paradigm

Let's talk about something that's near and dear to all of our hearts: power. No, I don't mean the 'become a supervillain and take over the world' kind of power. I mean the power to control your own destiny, especially financially. That's where Bitcoin and its ilk come storming in like a bull in a china shop—or a decentralized currency in a centralized world. Okay, I know that's not as catchy, but you get what I mean.

You see, Bitcoin isn't just a new way to pay for your morning cup of joe or a clever method to avoid overdraft fees. It's a tool for financial sovereignty. In places where governments are unstable, corrupt, or just plain negligent, Bitcoin offers an alternative. It's like financial punk rock, resisting the mainstream institutions that have kept people in check for so long. People can hold their heads high, knowing they don't have to rely on a bank or a governing body to control their financial future. They're the captains of their own fiscal ships.

And it's not just about the individual. Oh no, my friend. This is bigger. It's about emerging markets, too. In countries where inflation rates look like phone numbers (you know who you are, Zimbabwe), Bitcoin offers a lifeboat in a sea of economic turmoil. It allows businesses to operate with less friction, helps people preserve their savings, and creates opportunities for new kinds of commerce. In places where traditional financial systems have failed, cryptocurrency is stepping in to level the playing field. It's not a silver bullet, but it sure is a shiny one.

But wait, there's more. Ever heard of social movements being funded through Bitcoin? You betcha! When you can send financial aid halfway across the world in the blink of an eye, and without bureaucratic red tape, you're empowering people in a way that was not possible before. It's like being able to teleport supplies into a besieged city. The immediacy and autonomy that Bitcoin offers make it an invaluable tool for activism and humanitarian efforts. Talk about changing the world one block (chain) at a time.

Of course, we can't talk about Bitcoin's societal impact without discussing its cultural significance. This is a currency, a technology, and a movement all rolled into one. It has spawned a legion of die-hard fans, skeptics, and curious onlookers. Bitcoin has its own lexicon, memes, and even holidays (Bitcoin Pizza Day, anyone?). It's as much a part of today's zeitgeist as avocado toast and TikTok dances.

The cultural shift toward a decentralized economy challenges long-standing norms. We're starting to question why things have to be the way they are. Why do we need banks to hold our money? Why should governments have a monopoly on currency? In a decentralized world, power structures are flattened, and the middlemen are given a run for their money—literally.

Last but not least, let's touch on politics. Ah yes, the subject everyone loves to argue about at family dinners. Bitcoin intersects with politics in fascinating ways, from lawmakers grappling with how to regulate it to political campaigns accepting Bitcoin donations. Whether you're a libertarian praising the virtues of a decentralized economy or a regulator wary of potential illicit uses, Bitcoin doesn't care about your political leanings. It just keeps on doing its thing—empowering people, disrupting systems, and sparking debate.

So, as you dig deeper into the Bitcoin universe, take a moment to ponder its broader implications. You're not just investing in a currency or a technology; you're buying a ticket to a financial revolution that's shaking the very core of society and culture. It's a ride you won't want to miss.

Chapter 18:

Future Predictions: What Experts Say About Bitcoin's Potential

Ah, the future! A realm of endless possibilities, from flying cars to vacation homes on Mars. Just like we wonder about those sci-fi dreams, we can't help but speculate about the future of Bitcoin. So, strap on your seatbelts, or rocket boosters, as we journey through time to explore what experts are saying about where Bitcoin is headed.

First off, let's talk about the pros—the people who are so bullish on Bitcoin, you'd think they were talking about a golden goose that lays diamond eggs. According to these optimistic wizards of Wall Street and Silicon Valley, Bitcoin is on track to replace gold, outshine the dollar, and become the digital store of value for the future. These folks point to its fixed supply, growing adoption, and revolutionary technology as reasons for its inevitable skyrocket. If you ask them, they'll tell you to "buy the dip," "hold on for dear life," and prepare for a journey to the moon—or maybe even further, who knows?

On the flip side, we have the bears—the Grinches who apparently want to rain on our parade. They point out concerns like scalability, volatile prices, and regulatory uncertainties. They're the ones who fill your Twitter feed with doom and gloom, cautioning that Bitcoin is nothing more than a speculative bubble, a fad as transient as pet rocks or Beanie Babies. According to these naysayers, you'd best be prepared for a harsh landing back on Earth. Ah well, to each their own!

So, what does all this mean for the future of finance? If the bulls have their way, we'll all be transacting in Bitcoin while traditional banks scurry around like Blockbuster when Netflix came into play. But if the bears are right, then perhaps Bitcoin will remain a niche asset, like an exotic collector's item—coveted but not quite essential. Either way, the very conversations we're having about Bitcoin are slowly reshaping the way we think about money, and that, my friends, is nothing short of revolutionary.

Now, what about the tech? Oh, the sweet, sweet advancements that are cooking up in crypto kitchens around the globe. We're talking about developments like the Lightning Network for faster transactions and Taproot for enhanced privacy and smart contracts. These innovations have the potential to make Bitcoin more user-friendly, more functional, and just downright more awesome. Think of it as getting a software update that turns your regular old car into a self-driving, voice-activated wonder machine.

Last but not least, let's talk about the regulatory crystal ball. Governments worldwide are figuring out how to cope with this wild child of the financial world. In some countries, like El Salvador, Bitcoin has been welcomed with open arms and even adopted as legal tender. In others, it's viewed with suspicion, leading to regulatory crackdowns. But here's the kicker: the more governments try to regulate it, the more people want to know about it. It's like the Streisand effect for the digital age.

To sum it all up, the future of Bitcoin is as clear as mud. It could shoot up like a rocket or fizzle out like a wet firework. But if there's one thing we've learned from this roller coaster ride, it's that Bitcoin is not for the faint of heart. It's a high-stakes game that has captivated the minds of everyone, from Wall Street hotshots to basement-dwelling tech enthusiasts.

So, whether you're a bull or a bear, a tech geek or a finance guru, Bitcoin promises an exciting, albeit uncertain, journey into the future. And like any great story, the ending is still unwritten. But one thing's for sure: it's going to be a page-turner, and you won't want to miss a single chapter.

Chapter 19:

Action Plan: Your Roadmap to Becoming a Bitcoin Millionaire

Welcome to the pièce de résistance of our crypto journey—the part where we roll up our sleeves, snap on some gloves, and dig into the nitty-gritty of making our Bitcoin dreams come true. Let's talk about how to plot your course toward becoming a Bitcoin millionaire—or at least someone who can confidently throw around words like "blockchain" and "Satoshi" at cocktail parties.

First up, we're diving into the deep pool of financial goal-setting. Oh, I can hear your groans, but hear me out. How will you know you've arrived if you don't even know where you're going? So, sit down and ask yourself: "Self, what do I want to achieve with Bitcoin?" Whether it's a secure retirement, a new car, or simply bragging rights, having a clear destination will help you stay the course when the going gets tough—and in the Bitcoin world, it often does.

Now that you've got your eyes on the prize, let's chat about budgets and investment plans. You know how we all love impulse shopping? Well, let's just say that impulse investing in Bitcoin can have far-reaching consequences, and not the good kind. Work out how much you can comfortably invest without affecting your current lifestyle. We're talking about disposable income, not the money earmarked for rent or your grandma's birthday gift. Then decide how you'll allocate these funds: Will you go all-in on Bitcoin, or will you diversify with some altcoins or even traditional investments?

Next on our action-packed agenda is the strategy update. Let's face it, the crypto market is as stable as a Jenga tower five moves away from toppling. You'll need to keep your strategy flexible and up-to-date. Make it a habit to review your investment plan, say, once a month or after major market shifts. This isn't set-and-forget like that weird chia pet you got last Christmas; this requires regular TLC.

Of course, you can't revise your strategy without staying in the loop. You'll need to be more glued to market trends and news than a teenager is to their smartphone. Subscribe to newsletters, stalk forums, and maybe even set Google Alerts for Bitcoin news. The more you know, the better you'll navigate through the maze of misinformation, FUD (Fear, Uncertainty, Doubt), and FOMO (Fear Of Missing Out) that comes with the crypto territory.

Finally, let's add a dash of social spice to your crypto life by building a network of like-minded investors. I'm not talking about that weird cousin who keeps trying to get you to invest in his "revolutionary" startup; I mean people who genuinely share your passion for Bitcoin. Attend meetups, join online communities, and consider forming or joining an investment group. Your future self will thank you when you have a cadre of crypto friends to celebrate or commiserate with, depending on where the Bitcoin roller coaster takes you next.

To sum it all up: aim high but plan carefully, invest wisely, stay updated, and make friends along the way. This roadmap doesn't guarantee you'll become a Bitcoin millionaire overnight—let's leave the instant gratification to instant noodles. But it does promise you a fulfilling, educational, and possibly lucrative adventure in the world of cryptocurrency.

And there we have it, folks! Your action plan, your blueprint, your treasure map to potentially hitting that sweet, sweet seven-figure status—or at least to being the coolest crypto geek on the block. Now go forth and conquer, and may your future be as shiny as a newly minted Bitcoin!

Conclusion: Reshaping Your Financial Destiny with Bitcoin

Well, well, well. Look at you, all grown up, ready to reshape your financial destiny with Bitcoin. You've scaled the peaks of blockchain knowledge, swam through the murky waters of crypto scams, and even dabbled in the fine art of HODLing. I'd say you've earned a breather—maybe a tropical vacation paid for in Bitcoin?

Before you sprint off to implement all these marvelous strategies and tips, let's stroll down memory lane and recap what we've journeyed through together. We started off skeptical, maybe even clueless, but look at us now—well-versed in everything from smart contracts to cold storage solutions. If that isn't transformative, I don't know what is.

Remember how we talked about Bitcoin's revolutionary potential? We delved into how it's disrupting the financial sector, enabling financial inclusion, and even powering new forms of art through NFTs. Bitcoin isn't just another buzzword; it's a paradigm shift, a game-changer that has the potential to redefine how we interact with money and beyond.

So, what does the future hold? I could don my wizard hat and peer into a crystal ball, but the truth is, no one really knows. However, I can say this: The future is likely to be as unpredictable as a cat on catnip. There'll be ups, downs, and maybe a few loop-de-loops, but that's what makes it an adventure, right? With the foundational knowledge you've gained from this book, you'll be well-equipped to navigate whatever the crypto universe throws your way.

Now, let's talk about taking those crucial first steps. Like any journey, the first step is often the most daunting. You'll be tempted to put it off, maybe indulge in a little procrastination—binge-watch a series or reorganize your sock drawer. Resist the urge! Take one tiny step, whether it's setting up your first Bitcoin wallet or making a minuscule investment, it doesn't matter. A step is a step, and it's always in the right direction.

And, let's not forget—you're not going at it alone. You've got a wealth of resources at your fingertips and a community of crypto enthusiasts who are just as eager to reshape their financial destiny. Heck, you've got me, in spirit, nudging you along, reminding you to never ignore those red flags and always back up your wallet!

Which brings me to my last point—thank you. A heartfelt, over-the-moon thank you for letting me be a part of your crypto journey. We've laughed, we've pondered, and maybe, just maybe, we've experienced a couple of "Aha!" moments together. It's been a joy and a privilege, and I couldn't have asked for a better traveling companion on this wild ride through the crypto cosmos.

So here's to you, reshaping your financial destiny one block—pun totally intended—at a time. May your wallets be ever secure, your investments ever fruitful, and your spirit ever adventurous. Go forth and seize the decentralized day, knowing you're armed with the knowledge, tools, and dad jokes necessary to thrive in this brave new world of Bitcoin.

In the words of the unknown poet—well, actually just me a few moments ago—your future is as shiny as a newly minted Bitcoin.

Signing off, but never really gone. After all, we're all just a blockchain link in this grand tapestry of crypto life.

And that's a wrap! The ball's in your court now. I hope you're as excited to dive deeper into the world of Bitcoin as I am to hear about your future triumphs. Until then, keep it crypto!

Chapter 20:

Embracing the Crypto Lifestyle: Beyond Just Bitcoin

Ah, the crypto world! It's not just a field of finance; it's an exciting realm, a community, and above all, a lifestyle. One does not simply "buy Bitcoin". No, delving into cryptocurrency is akin to stepping into a parallel universe where conventional finance conventions get a delightful twist, where your allegiance to a token might rival the fervor for a favorite sports team, and where the mighty meme can morph into monetary magic.

Embarking on this crypto journey, it soon becomes evident that this world is vast, dynamic, and incredibly diverse. Sure, Bitcoin rings a bell for many, but have you heard the tales of Dogecoin? The cheeky coin, conceived as a joke, not only had its moment under the spotlight but also received nods from tech giants like Elon Musk. And if you think that's bizarre, welcome to Decentraland, where virtual real estate trades happen through cryptocurrencies. Wait, there's more! The wave of DeFi, or decentralized finance, is on the horizon, challenging the traditional banking goliaths and promising a redefined financial landscape. This isn't a mere fleeting trend; it's a testament to the expansive nature of the crypto realm.

But coins, tokens, and finance aside, the true essence of the crypto lifestyle is the vibrant culture it encapsulates.

Joining this movement means becoming part of a global brigade, questioning and revolutionizing the established norms. Imagine flaunting a 'HODL' tee, not as a misspelled fashion statement, but as a testament to your unwavering faith in the tumultuous world of crypto. This lifestyle is about connections, both virtual and real, where brainstorming sessions happen over digital conferences or at local coffee shop meetups. It's where ideas, strategies, and yes, even the latest dank memes, are fervently exchanged.

However, every silver lining has its cloud. The same adrenaline-pumping volatility that makes crypto so enticing can also churn stomachs when market graphs take a nosedive. For newcomers, the sheer plethora of coins available can be daunting – imagine being a child, nose pressed against the candy store window, indecision at its peak. And the debates, oh boy! Technical intricacies like Proof of Work versus Proof of Stake or the merits and demerits of centralized versus decentralized exchanges can fuel discussions so intense they'd put political debates to shame.

So, as an aspiring crypto aficionado, how does one navigate this intricate maze? The answer lies in a blend of continuous learning, strategic diversification, and a pinch of audacity.

Being in the crypto world is synonymous with perpetual learning. Given the rapid advancements, staying updated is more a necessity than a choice. Whether you scour crypto news portals, engage in enlightening forum debates, or seek insights from seasoned influencers (the genuine ones, not the hype merchants), ensure you're always in the know.

While having a favorite coin is great, it's crucial not to let biases cloud judgment. The age-old wisdom of not putting all eggs in one basket is gold in the crypto universe. Bitcoin, while being the undisputed monarch, is not the sole player. The crypto terrain is teeming with potential gems. So, dive deep, research with gusto, and spread your investments.

But most importantly, remember to relish this roller-coaster ride. The crypto voyage is nothing if not unpredictable, with its exhilarating peaks and daunting troughs. Celebrate those soaring moments, introspect during downturns, and always keep in mind that whether you're here for the groundbreaking technology, the tantalizing profits, or just the sheer thrill, you're at the forefront of a monumental shift.

Embracing the crypto lifestyle is certainly not for the feeble-hearted. It requires resilience, adaptability, and a dash of daring. But if you've ventured this far, you're clearly cut out for it. So, fasten your seatbelts, delve deep, and let your crypto journey be as enthralling as it is prosperous!

Chapter 21:

NFTs - The New Digital Art Revolution

Once upon a time, in a world not too dissimilar to ours, the idea of owning a unique piece of digital art was laughed at. "Digital?" they'd scoff, "Surely you can just copy and paste it!" But, as with all great tales, along came a hero to change the narrative. Enter NFTs, or Non-Fungible Tokens, riding on the back of a dragon named Blockchain, and the realm of digital art would never be the same again.

So, what exactly are these magical NFTs? In simple terms, NFTs represent a one-of-a-kind digital asset, verified using blockchain technology. Imagine having an autographed poster of your favorite celebrity. Sure, there are thousands of posters out there, but yours has that special signature making it unique. NFTs are the digital equivalent of that autograph, signifying your exclusive ownership of a piece of digital art or collectible.

Their rise in the world of art has been nothing short of meteoric. Digital artists, once overshadowed by their canvas-touting counterparts, found a new, lucrative platform. Celebrities jumped aboard too, minting tweets, songs, and even moments. It felt like everyone and their dog (or should we say, Doge?) wanted a slice of the NFT pie.

But let's rewind a tad. How does all this work? It's our trusty steed, the blockchain, that ensures the authenticity and uniqueness of every NFT. Each token is stamped with a unique code, stored on a decentralized network. This ensures that while someone might "right-click-save" a digital artwork, they won't own the original NFT or its associated bragging rights.

Now, you might wonder how these differ from other cryptocurrencies like Bitcoin. Well, while tokens like Bitcoin are 'fungible' and can be exchanged on a one-for-one basis, NFTs are 'non-fungible.' Think of it like exchanging a ten-dollar bill for two fives. That's fungibility. But with NFTs, each one is distinct, much like trading cards. No two are the same, even if they look alike.

Ready to dive in? Platforms like OpenSea, Rarible, and Foundation have become the bustling bazaars for NFT trade. Whether you're an artist, a collector, or just curious, these platforms allow for the creation, purchase, and sale of these unique tokens.

However, as with all things shiny and new, there's a flip side. The environmental impact of NFTs has raised eyebrows. The immense energy required by the computers upholding the blockchain is equivalent to the power consumed by some small countries. Yet, the community is aware and is making strides toward greener solutions.

Beyond art, NFTs are making touchdowns in sports, hitting high notes in music, and rolling out the red carpet in entertainment. From NBA Top Shots capturing iconic game moments to musicians selling albums as NFTs, the applications seem boundless.

But what does this mean for the future of digital ownership? We're entering an era where owning a digital item gives as much satisfaction, if not more, as owning a physical one. Your virtual sneaker collection or digital concert tickets might just be as prized as your signed memorabilia.

Valuing NFTs, however, is a blend of art and science. Some fetch millions, while others, just a few bucks. Their value hinges on factors like the artist's reputation, the item's historical significance, and, let's be honest, a good dose of market hype.

Yet, as NFTs dance in the limelight, not everyone's applauding. Critics argue it's a bubble, a fad that'll soon pop. Some see it as a playground for the rich, while others question the longevity of digital ownership. But whether you're an NFT aficionado or a skeptic, one thing's for sure: they've sparked a conversation that's echoing across the art halls and digital forums alike.

Will NFTs continue to be the poster child of the digital art revolution, or will they fade into the annals of internet history? Only time will tell. But for now, as we stand at the crossroads of art, technology, and commerce, it's a thrilling time to be alive. So, keep your eyes peeled, your crypto-wallet handy, and who knows? The next digital Mona Lisa could be just a click away!

Chapter 22:

DeFi - The Future of Decentralized Finance

Step aside traditional finance, there's a new kid on the block! And this one doesn't wear a suit or need a flashy office skyscraper. Welcome to the world of DeFi, or Decentralized Finance, which is stirring up quite the buzz in financial circles and beyond. It's like the punk rock of the finance world, disruptive yet full of potential.

DeFi is not just a fancy acronym but represents a radical rethinking of financial systems. It's the notion that financial services from lending to insurance can be provided without a central authority, like banks or brokers, in the mix. Imagine having a global financial system where anyone, regardless of their socioeconomic status or geographic location, can access services without the need for intermediaries. A financial system where you, the user, have full control over your assets. That's the magic DeFi promises to bring to the table.

At the heart of this revolution lies the principle that technology, specifically blockchain technology, can replace these intermediaries. It's like firing the middleman and replacing him with lines of code. Sounds weird? Maybe. But it's precisely what makes DeFi so exciting. It aims to provide a more transparent, accessible, and inclusive financial system.

Perhaps you're wondering how all of this works. The magic word here is "smart contracts." Not contracts written with fancy pens, but self-executing contracts with terms directly written into lines of code. They automatically execute actions when certain conditions are met, without the need for a trusted third party. It's like having a robot lawyer and banker rolled into one, tirelessly working on the blockchain.

There's a dazzling array of DeFi protocols out there, each with its unique approach. From Compound, which lets you earn interest on your crypto, to MakerDAO, where you can take out a loan without a credit check. And the beauty of it? They operate round the clock, without holidays or lunch breaks!

One term you might have heard floating around DeFi circles is "yield farming." It's not about growing crops, but about smartly navigating the DeFi space to harvest the best interest rates. By providing liquidity or participating in a DeFi protocol, users can earn rewards. It's a bit like choosing which bank to put your money in based on the interest they offer, but on steroids.

However, before you dive headfirst into this world, it's essential to understand that DeFi isn't without its risks. The decentralized nature means fewer safety nets. There have been instances of scams and hacks. And then there's the complex beast called "impermanent loss" which can occur when providing liquidity in certain DeFi protocols. It's always essential to do your homework and perhaps not put all your crypto eggs in one DeFi basket.

And what does the mighty hand of regulation have to say about all this? Well, DeFi's decentralized nature poses quite a challenge for regulators. How do you regulate something that doesn't have a central governing body? The tussle between innovation and regulation will be interesting to watch, with both sides having valid concerns.

One can't discuss DeFi without touching upon its potential impact on the world's banking systems. Some enthusiasts believe DeFi could make traditional banks obsolete. Why rely on a bank when you can take out a decentralized loan on your terms? However, others argue that banks and DeFi can coexist, each serving different needs and audiences. Only time will tell which vision pans out.

DeFi has given birth to some fascinating use cases. Decentralized exchanges (or DEXs for short) like Uniswap allow users to trade without a central authority. Think of them as the eBay of crypto, connecting buyers and sellers directly. Then there's decentralized insurance, giving users a way to hedge against risks without insurance companies. And we're just scratching the surface here. The possibilities seem endless.

Considering the rapid growth and development in the DeFi sector, one can't help but feel optimistic. While it's still in its infancy, the trajectory points towards a future where finance is more open, transparent, and democratized. The innovations we're seeing today might just be the tip of the iceberg.

To wrap it up, DeFi is an exciting, albeit complex, frontier in the world of finance. It challenges the very foundations of traditional financial systems, promising a world where financial services are more accessible and equitable. Whether you're a crypto enthusiast, a skeptic, or just plain curious, there's no denying that DeFi is a space to watch. After all, who knows? The next big financial revolution might just be a blockchain away!

Chapter 23:

The Evolution of Digital Identity

As the digital era transforms every facet of our lives, our identity in this expansive virtual space becomes essential. Welcome to the captivating world of digital identity, where technology not only knows your name but also understands the vast tapestry of data woven around it.

Digital Identity and Its Significance

Imagine a world where a single digital profile represents you, encompassing everything from your passport details to your last online purchase. That's the essence of digital identity. It's the online equivalent of who we are in the physical world. Given our increasing reliance on online services, from social media to online banking, having a secure and trustworthy digital ID is paramount. This ensures not just convenience but also security in an age of cyber threats.

The Quagmire of Online Identity Verification

However, it's not all smooth sailing in the world of digital identity. Our current systems are fragmented. You might have one password for your email, another for your social media, and yet another for your online banking. And then there's the dreaded password reset when you inevitably forget one! Beyond just the inconvenience, there's a grave concern for security. With multiple identities and passwords across platforms, vulnerabilities arise, often leading to breaches and identity theft.

Blockchain to the Rescue

Here's where the magic of blockchain comes into play. With its immutable and decentralized ledger, blockchain has the potential to consolidate and securely manage digital identities. Imagine a world where you control your digital identity, stored securely on a blockchain, and can provide access to services as and when needed. No more juggling multiple passwords, no more fretting over potential breaches. Just a seamless, secure digital life.

Enter the Self-Sovereign Identity

In the blockchain world, there's a buzz about self-sovereign identity. It's an empowering concept where you, and only you, have control over your personal data. Instead of entrusting your details to various service providers, you hold the keys. Need to verify your age for a service? Instead of handing over your entire ID card details, you'd simply provide a digital proof. Your data remains with you, shared only on a need-to-know basis.

Digital ID in Action

The implications of a robust digital identity system are profound. Imagine casting your vote in national elections from the comfort of your home, safe in the knowledge that your identity is secure and your vote counts. In healthcare, medical records can be stored and shared securely, ensuring you receive personalized care wherever you go. Travelling becomes a breeze with digital IDs speeding up verification processes. And for the unbanked population worldwide, digital identity could be the passport to financial services, fostering global financial inclusion.

Cybersecurity and Digital Identity: Two Sides of the Same Coin

An effective digital ID system isn't just about convenience; it's also a formidable weapon in the cybersecurity arsenal. With each user having a unique, verifiable, and immutable digital identity, hackers would find it increasingly challenging to perpetrate fraud, ensuring our online interactions remain safe.

Governments and the Digital ID Dance

While the concept sounds futuristic, many governments are already exploring digital ID systems, recognizing their potential. Estonia, for instance, is a pioneer in this space. However, integrating digital IDs at a national or global level is complex. It promises streamlined services but also raises concerns, particularly around surveillance and misuse.

Thwarting Online Fraudsters

One of the most compelling cases for digital IDs is their potential to combat online fraud. Identity theft and online scams have burgeoned in the digital age. By providing a verifiable and secure digital identity for every user, the tables can turn, making online fraud increasingly untenable.

Walking the Ethical Tightrope

However, as with any revolutionary concept, there are challenges. Chief among these is the ethical consideration of data privacy. In an era where data is the new oil, who truly owns our digital identity? The allure of data monetization is massive. Hence, as we tread this path, ensuring ethical usage and robust data privacy becomes paramount.

In wrapping up our deep dive into digital identity, it's clear that the evolution of how we see and secure ourselves in the digital realm is at a fascinating crossroad. As technology advances and intertwines further with our daily lives, the call for a consolidated, secure, and user-controlled digital identity will only grow louder. The future beckons, and it promises to be a world where our digital self is as rich, secure, and recognized as our physical self.

Chapter 24:

Central Bank Digital Currencies (CBDCs) - The State's Response

Pull up a comfy chair and get cozy, because today, we're diving into a topic that's as tantalizing as the latest detective novel: Central Bank Digital Currencies, or CBDCs for short. If you've been wondering how the big wigs at central banks have been reacting to the whirlwind that is cryptocurrency, then boy, have you come to the right place!

Imagine, for a moment, a world where you can pay for your morning coffee using a digital currency issued by your country's central bank. Sounds futuristic, doesn't it? Well, with CBDCs, that future might just be around the corner.

Now, you might be asking, "Aren't CBDCs just like our beloved Bitcoin or Ethereum?" Well, not exactly. While both are digital, CBDCs are state-sponsored, meaning they have a country's official stamp of approval. Think of them as the digital equivalent of the banknotes in your wallet, but with a dash of technological magic.

"Why are nations so keen on this?" you ponder. Well, there's a potpourri of reasons. For starters, CBDCs can give policymakers a new toolkit for their monetary policies. They can help central banks implement interest rates more effectively, especially in a world flirting with negative interest rates. Moreover, with everything going digital, it seems only fitting for money to get a tech makeover too.

CBDCs could also enhance financial stability. Think of times when panic strikes, and everyone rushes to withdraw money. With CBDCs, central banks can ensure liquidity is always available, calming those financial jitters.

Behind the curtain of these CBDCs is, of course, some cutting-edge tech. While not all use blockchain, the technology that underpins cryptocurrencies, some indeed do. The choice of technology often depends on the goals of the particular central bank and the trade-offs they're willing to make.

Speaking of pioneers in this realm, a few countries are already strutting their stuff. China, for example, has been testing its Digital Yuan in various cities. The Bahamas has its Sand Dollar, and Sweden's been playing around with the e-Krona. Each of these trailblazers is exploring CBDCs in their unique way, setting the stage for the future of digital currencies.

One of the juiciest prospects of CBDCs is their potential to make cross-border transactions smoother than a freshly churned milkshake. We're talking about faster, cheaper, and more efficient international payments. This is a game-changer, especially for countries that heavily rely on remittances.

But, and there's always a "but", isn't there? There are privacy concerns. CBDCs, being state-sponsored, could allow governments to keep tabs on every transaction you make. This Big Brother-esque scenario raises questions: How much surveillance is too much? Can we ensure anonymity and, at the same time, prevent illicit activities?

Moreover, if everyone starts using CBDCs, where does that leave our dear old commercial banks? With the ability to have an account directly with the central bank, some traditional banking functions might need a revamp or risk becoming obsolete. This could reshape the financial landscape in ways we've not yet fully grasped.

It's also worth noting that CBDCs aren't just being developed for fun. They are, in part, a response to the growing popularity of cryptocurrencies. If you can't beat them, join them, right? Governments see the writing on the digital wall and understand the need to modernize and adapt.

Yet, like any blockbuster story, there are challenges and potential plot twists. Technical issues, security concerns, and the mammoth task of integrating CBDCs into existing financial systems are just a few of the hurdles. And let's not forget the naysayers, predicting that CBDCs might just be a passing phase.

So, what's in the crystal ball for CBDCs? While it's tricky to predict the exact trajectory, it's evident that they're more than just a fleeting fancy. As technology evolves and the kinks get ironed out, CBDCs might just become a staple in our financial diet.

In wrapping up, think of CBDCs as the latest act in the grand play of finance. They're the state's response to a world that's rapidly digitizing. Whether they end up being the hero or the villain (or a bit of both) in our story remains to be seen. So, grab your popcorn and watch this space!

Chapter 25:

The Role of Cryptocurrencies in Philanthropy

Cue the spotlight, bring out the violin, and let's address the softer side of the crypto world. No, it's not about another Doge meme (though those are quite delightful), but about something more heartwarming – cryptocurrencies and their budding romance with philanthropy.

Imagine this: It's a quiet evening, and you're scrolling through your crypto portfolio. Among the green and red market percentages, a thought dawns upon you – "What if I could use this digital gold to make the world a better place?" Welcome to the beautiful convergence of crypto and charity.

The realm of charitable giving has been having a little love affair with cryptocurrency. It's like when peanut butter met jelly or when Netflix met chill. More and more philanthropists are opting to donate in Bitcoin, Ethereum, and the like. And why not? Cryptocurrencies, with their decentralized nature, can offer a level of transparency that's like a breath of fresh air. Donors can track their funds, ensuring that their generous contributions are being used as intended, all thanks to the wondrous blockchain technology. Gone are the days of wondering if that donation ended up buying a fancy chandelier for a CEO's office instead of drilling a well in a parched village.

But wait, there's more! If you're ever in need of some dinner party chatter, try this: "Did you know donating in crypto can be tax-efficient?" That's right! Many countries offer tax incentives for charitable donations, and crypto is no exception. In fact, donating cryptocurrency might help dodge those pesky capital gains taxes. Of course, always consult with a tax professional, but it's a neat little perk for those with benevolent intentions.

Now, if you're wondering which charitable organizations are riding the crypto wave, you might be pleasantly surprised. Renowned entities, from UNICEF to The Water Project, have warmed up to the idea of receiving cryptocurrencies. They're like the cool grandparents who are totally up-to-date with the latest tech trends.

And when calamity strikes? That's when crypto truly shines. In times of disasters, the need for swift aid is paramount. With crypto's rapid transfer capabilities, relief can be dispatched promptly, making a tangible difference in real-time. No waiting for bank clearances or wading through bureaucratic muddles.

The global impact of such crypto kindness is nothing short of transformative. Charities can now tap into a global donor base, unfettered by currency restrictions or international fees. It's like opening the gates of generosity, where a coder in Silicon Valley can effortlessly fund a classroom in a remote African village.

However, every rose has its thorn, and crypto-philanthropy is no different. The volatile nature of cryptocurrencies can be a double-edged sword. Imagine donating an amount one day, only to find its value plummet the next. Then there's the ever-evolving landscape of crypto regulations, which can sometimes feel like trying to pin jelly to a wall. And let's not even get started on the intricacies of converting large sums of crypto to fiat money. It's enough to give anyone a mild headache.

But wait, the plot thickens! Enter the world of charitable trusts with a crypto twist. These are exciting new frontiers where the traditional meets the futuristic. Trusts that can hold cryptocurrencies are becoming a reality, providing another avenue for long-term charitable endeavors.

Speaking of futuristic, smart contracts are set to play leading roles in ensuring donation efficiency. Picture this: A smart contract that automatically allocates funds to a project once certain conditions are met, ensuring timely and effective use of donations. It's like having a digital genie overseeing philanthropic wishes.

So, what does the crystal ball hold for the union of crypto and charity? To put it mildly, the prospects are dazzling. As more people embrace cryptocurrencies and their potential, it's only natural for this warmth to spill over into altruistic endeavors. The decentralized, transparent, and global nature of crypto makes it an ideal match for the ever-evolving world of philanthropy.

In the grand tapestry of the crypto universe, amidst tales of fortunes made and lost, lies this gentle thread of philanthropy, shimmering with hope and kindness. It's a testament to the human spirit, a reminder that amidst the chaos of numbers and charts, there's room for heart, for compassion, for change.

As we close this chapter, take a moment to reflect. In the vast digital cosmos, each of us has the power to be a beacon of change, to use our digital treasures to carve out a legacy of kindness. Because, at the end of the day, it's not just about how much crypto you have, but how you choose to use it. Here's to a future where the blockchain doesn't just store transactions but also the echoes of our benevolence. Cheers to that!

Conclusion:

Reshaping Your Financial Destiny with Bitcoin

Well, here we are at the end of our crypto rollercoaster, and what a thrilling ride it's been! If you're feeling a tad dizzy from all the twists and turns, don't worry—you're not alone. The world of Bitcoin is nothing short of a head-spinning wonderland.

Let's take a moment to reflect on the key gems we've unearthed together throughout this journey. Remember when we unpacked the genesis of Bitcoin? Ah, it feels like just a few pages ago we were naively venturing into this digital realm, and now, look at you—practically a Bitcoin sage ready to regale friends and family with tales of blockchains and Satoshi Nakamoto.

We've discussed at length Bitcoin's transformative potential. It's not merely a flashy digital asset or a modern-day gold rush. It's an innovative piece of tech wizardry poised to redefine the way we perceive, use, and manage money. It's a rebellion against traditional financial systems, a promise of decentralized power, and above all, an open invitation for everyone (yes, everyone!) to hop on this financial freedom train. Who knew a string of digital code could hold so much promise and power?

As we ventured deeper into the book, we recognized that the value of Bitcoin isn't just its price ticker but also its potential to remodel our financial systems. A trustless, decentralized system that ensures security, transparency, and control? Now that's what we call a financial makeover!

Now, about the future—oh, if only we had a crypto crystal ball! But, even without it, it's evident that we're on the brink of something monumental. The Bitcoin wave isn't just coming—it's already here, crashing on the shores of traditional finance, and reshaping landscapes. We're not just talking about buying coffee with Bitcoin (though that's cool too) but about the broader societal shifts. As decentralized finance gains traction, it's paving the way for more open, accessible, and egalitarian financial structures.

Feeling excited? Good! But, as with everything splendid and shiny, it's essential to remember the foundational principles and do the necessary homework. You know the drill: research, diversify, never invest more than you can afford to lose, and always—always—keep your crypto keys safe. It's a wild world out there, but with the right knowledge (which you now possess, thanks to this book!), it's a lot less daunting.

Now, for the most crucial bit: taking the first step. Remember that every crypto guru, every Bitcoin millionaire, and every blockchain whiz started precisely where you are now—with curiosity and a desire to understand. The next step is to act. Dive in, start small, and remember, the crypto journey is as much about learning and evolving as it is about potential profits.

Before we part ways, let's get a tad sentimental, shall we? A colossal thank-you is in order. Thank you for embarking on this journey, for turning every page with enthusiasm, and for allowing this book to be your guide in the vast world of Bitcoin. Your engagement, dear explorer, has made every word worth writing.

So, here we are, at the precipice of new beginnings. The world of Bitcoin awaits, filled with endless possibilities and opportunities. Whether you're in it for the thrill, the profit, or the sheer love of disruptive tech, there's a place for you in this crypto cosmos. As you step forth, remember the lessons, cherish the knowledge, and always keep that infectious curiosity alive.

To Bitcoin and beyond, may your financial horizons be forever expansive and bright! Safe travels on your crypto journey, and until our paths cross again, happy hodling!

Appendix A:

Glossary of Bitcoin and Cryptocurrency Terms

Ah, welcome to the treasure trove of crypto-speak! If you've been reading this book and scratching your head thinking, "What in Satoshi's name does that mean?", then you've come to the right place. This glossary is like the crypto dictionary, a sidekick that explains all the jargony stuff. No cape required, though feel free to don one for added flair.

Altcoins: You know the phrase, "There's plenty of fish in the sea"? Well, think of Bitcoin as the Great White Shark, and all the other smaller fish as altcoins. These are alternative cryptocurrencies to Bitcoin, trying to make their own splash.

Blockchain: Picture a digital ledger, but instead of being guarded by goblins in a magical bank, it's stored on computers all over the world. Each "block" of data gets added to a long "chain." Thus, blockchain.

Cold Storage: No, it's not where you keep your ice cream. It's a way to store your crypto offline, away from the hungry eyes of hackers.

Decentralization: Imagine a world where no single entity rules. Instead, the power is distributed amongst its citizens—or in the case of Bitcoin, among various computers worldwide. No kings or queens, only a round table of equals.

Fork: Sorry, not the eating utensil. In the crypto world, a fork happens when there's a change in the blockchain's protocol, creating two different paths—one that follows the new protocol and one that sticks to the old.

HODL: A term of endearment for long-term holders of crypto. It started from a typo in an online forum, and the community just ran with it. It's essentially a battle cry for resisting the urge to sell when prices are down.

Mining: Not the pickaxe and helmet kind. It's the process of using computer power to solve complex equations, which in turn secures the blockchain and rewards you with some shiny new coins.

NFT: Stands for Non-Fungible Token. Unlike your everyday, run-of-the-mill cryptocurrencies, each NFT is unique. It's like owning a rare collectible action figure, but in digital form.

Private Key: Think of it as the magical spell that controls access to your treasure. Guard it with your life, or else someone might just Abracadabra your funds away.

Satoshi: Named after Bitcoin's mysterious creator, a Satoshi is the smallest unit of Bitcoin. It's like the penny to Bitcoin's dollar, except way, way smaller.

Smart Contracts: These are self-executing contracts where the terms are written in code. Imagine a vending machine: You insert a coin, make a selection, and out pops your snack. No middleman required.

2FA: Stands for Two-Factor Authentication. It's like having a secret handshake on top of a password. Makes it doubly hard for anyone to snoop around your accounts.

Wallet: Your digital purse, where you keep all your cryptocurrencies. Just don't leave it in a taxi; that could be...unfortunate.

Whale: In the ocean of crypto, a whale is someone who holds a massive amount of cryptocurrency. Their actions can make waves in the market, so keep an eye out!

Alright, my crypto-linguists, you've now been officially schooled in the ABCs (and DEFs and GHI's) of Bitcoin and cryptocurrency terms. Keep this glossary handy, and you'll be deciphering crypto jargon like it's your native tongue. Just don't start throwing around "HODL" and "blockchain" at family dinners, or you might have to start a glossary for them too.

There you have it! The jargon buster, the explainer-in-chief, your Appendix A. Who knew learning could be so fun, right?

Printed in Great Britain
by Amazon